National
Museums
Northern
Ireland

explore/engage/enjoy

TITANIC
Behind the Legend

William Blair
Head of Human History
National Museums Northern Ireland

ISBN 0 900761 55 5

Design: whitenoisestudios.com
Printed by: Nicholson & Bass

Cover image: This photograph, taken early March 1912, captures the last time that sister ships *Olympic* and *Titanic* were together. *Olympic* had returned to Harland & Wolff for repairs to a damaged propeller. This photograph shows *Olympic* (left) being manoeuvred into the flooded Thompson Graving Dock, with *Titanic* at the fitting-out wharf.
Inside flap front image: Promotional poster featuring *Olympic,* c. 1911.
Inside back flap image: Promotional postcard showing *Titanic.*
P.2-3 image: Harland & Wolff shipyard, Belfast, 1911

Contents

Foreword

The fateful tale of the maiden voyage of *Titanic* in April 1912 is one of the best-known stories in the world.

Less well-known is the dramatic story of how what was then the world's largest vessel came to be conceived and built in Belfast at the Harland & Wolff shipyard.

It is this story, and the story of the people who built *Titanic* and her sister ships *Olympic* and *Britannic*, which provides much of the focus of this book, 'Titanic – Behind The Legend'. Its text and images weave a remarkable narrative exploring the context of the ambitious design and build of these ships, the appeal and atmosphere of the transatlantic journey and the subsequent place of *Titanic* in myth and memory. It is a narrative which combines the best of human endeavour and the worst of human tragedy.

The author, William Blair (our Head of Human History), has been able to draw heavily from our rich national collections, accumulated with vision and with care across many years. The Ulster Folk and Transport Museum, part of National Museums Northern Ireland, is privileged to be the custodian of these collections. The museum is also blessed with a beautiful and relevant location on the shores of Belfast Lough. It was in these waters adjacent to the museum that *Titanic* was launched 100 years ago and from here that the great liner sailed to her place in history.

We are delighted through this publication to bring even more of our collections to public attention and to offer a fresh presentation of both the *Titanic* story and the wider story of Belfast's role at the heart of an astounding global enterprise.

Tim Cooke
Director
National Museums Northern Ireland

Design and Build

Oceanic, built by Harland & Wolff, made her maiden voyage in 1871 and was the first of many ships built for the White Star Line.

By 1900, Belfast had become one of the world's most prosperous industrial cities. It had the design skills and top quality workmanship to produce world-class steamships, despite having to import almost all of the raw materials for shipbuilding. Eleven years into the new century, *Titanic* was launched and in 1912 was lost on her maiden voyage – becoming the most famous ship in the world.

The story of *Titanic* is essentially the story of a close and fruitful working relationship between two companies: Harland & Wolff and the White Star Line.

The origins of the enterprising Harland & Wolff shipbuilding business lay in an ironworks owned by Robert Hickson in Eliza Street, Belfast. Producing more than the local market could absorb, Hickson decided to expand his business into shipbuilding on Queen's Island. As he knew nothing about the industry, he recruited a young shipbuilder named Edward Harland in 1854. From that year on grew an enterprise that would one day dominate world shipbuilding.

Thomas Ismay (1837-1899), founder of the White Star Line. He spent his lifetime building up the company to become one of the most important in the world.

Late 19th century watercolour of Belfast harbour by Mary Harland, sister of Edward Harland, co-founder of the Harland & Wolff shipyard in Belfast.

The powerful men who built up Harland & Wolff: (left to right) Gustav Wolff, W.H. Wilson, William J. Pirrie and Edward Harland. William Pirrie's energy and business acumen ensured that the firm prospered in the early years of the twentieth century.

Harland took over the business in 1858 and three years later formed a partnership with Gustav Wolff. From the start, the shipyard produced vessels that were built to the highest standards and with an admirable level of technical innovation. The yard's ship designs developed over the years and the designers were ever prepared to experiment with new concepts. For example, Harland & Wolff's first ship for the White Star Line was the elegant *Oceanic*, launched in 1871. Edward Harland's revolutionary design placed the Saloon (First Class) accommodation in the centre of the ship, rather than over the propellers at the stern. This provided a more comfortable voyage for passengers who were no longer affected by vibrations from the ship's screws. Other shipping lines subsequently followed this design.

The link with the White Star Line was crucial in the development of Harland & Wolff. The White Star Line had its origins in a shipping line that successfully operated sailing packets from Liverpool to Australia. When it failed in 1867, Liverpool-based Thomas Ismay purchased the company name and flag.

In 1869, Ismay founded the Oceanic Steam Navigation Company (the official name of the White Star Line) with William Imrie. Backed by financier Gustav Schwabe, the company entered the growing north Atlantic passenger trade. Schwabe's nephew, Gustav Wolff, was a partner with Edward Harland in the Belfast shipyard and Schwabe himself was a major shareholder in the yard. From 1869, Harland & Wolff built virtually all of the ships required by the White Star Line in a relationship that was to last over sixty years. This was a relationship built on trust. No contracts were ever signed: instead there was an agreement that a small profit would be

Teutonic, launched in 1889, was the first White Star Line vessel to be fitted with twin propellers and not to carry sails. Designed by Alexander Carlisle, the ship could be adapted for Admiralty use in wartime. *Teutonic* and her sister ship *Majestic* were stylish and popular with the travelling public. Both won the coveted 'Blue Riband' for the fastest crossing of the Atlantic.

added to the final total. This was termed 'cost plus'. It proved successful for both parties and allowed Harland & Wolff to expand and develop the shipyard over the decades.

As the White Star Line developed to cater for growing passenger markets, it regularly recommissioned vessels from Harland & Wolff. Between 1901 and 1907, Harland & Wolff built four large ships for the White Star Line: *Celtic (II)*, *Cedric*, *Baltic (II)* and *Adriatic (II)*. Designed for comfort and reliability, the popular 'Big Four' were the most important White Star Line ships in the years leading up to the construction of *Olympic*, *Titanic* and *Britannic*.

In 1906, the launch of the rival Cunard Line's huge fast ships *Lusitania* and *Mauretania* challenged the White Star Line for the lucrative and growing emigration business. The White Star Line was part of the International Mercantile Marine Company which was formed in 1902 by American financier J. Pierpont Morgan. His efforts to create a monopoly on north Atlantic shipping failed as some companies, notably Cunard, refused to join.

The second *Oceanic*, launched in 1899, was renowned for its size, comfort and luxurious accommodation.

In 1907, the White Star Line met the challenge of Cunard by deciding to construct three magnificent ships. Bruce Ismay, Chairman of the White Star Line, and William Pirrie, Chairman of Harland & Wolff, began to plan for the new vessels. The result was the construction in Belfast of the Olympic Class ships: *Olympic*, *Titanic* and *Britannic*.

Dignitaries on board *Teutonic* during the Naval Review at Spithead, off the Isle of Wight, on the occasion of Queen Victoria's Diamond Jubilee celebrations, 26 June 1897.

The elegant reading room on *Adriatic (II)*. On board luxury was a feature of many White Star Line vessels before the construction of the Olympic Class ships.

Emigrants from eastern Europe on board *Olympic* as she enters New York harbour, c.1911.

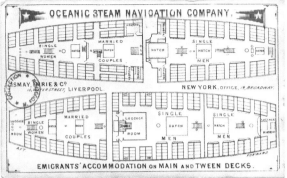

Card showing the *Adriatic (I)*, built by Harland & Wolff in 1872 for the White Star Line (Oceanic Steam Navigation Company). The back of the card shows emigrant accommodation on board the ship.

New arrivals at the Ellis Island Immigration Station in New York, early twentieth century.

Emigration

Emigration was the driving force behind the growth in demand for ocean transport in the late-nineteenth century. Millions of people left Europe to seek new lives in America and transporting them across the Atlantic became an increasingly important business.

As wooden sailing ships gave way to iron or steel hulled steamships, the length of the journey fell from approximately six weeks to about one week. Passenger legislation helped to improve travelling conditions for emigrants.

The White Star Line competed against its rivals to attract emigrants to its ships. It was a huge business: an average of nearly 900,000 immigrants entered the United States each year between 1900 and 1914.

High levels of emigration led to huge demand for transatlantic transport. The White Star Line helped emigrants by promotions such as special rates and through tickets to final destinations.

Inspection Card from 1904, stamped to show that the emigrant had entered the United States. Inspection Cards recorded the identity and health of those travelling in Third Class and were essential to allow them to land in the United States.

International Mercantile Marine Company

John Pierpont Morgan, with his trademark top hat, in New York c. 1910.

The White Star Line was part of the International Mercantile Marine Company (IMMC) between 1902 and 1927. The IMMC was formed by J. Pierpont Morgan who had built up an American steel, rail and banking empire. He aimed to dominate Atlantic shipping through this company. Bruce Ismay of the White Star Line served as IMMC President from 1904 to 1913. William Pirrie of Harland & Wolff was a director of IMMC, bringing valuable business to the shipyard.

'The splendid fleets of the International Mercantile Marine Company ply on all the Seven Seas.' Promotional brochure, c.1920.

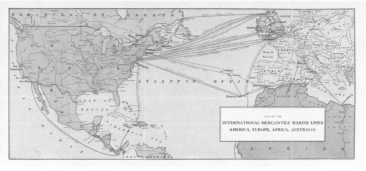

International Mercantile Marine Lines brochure, c. 1920.

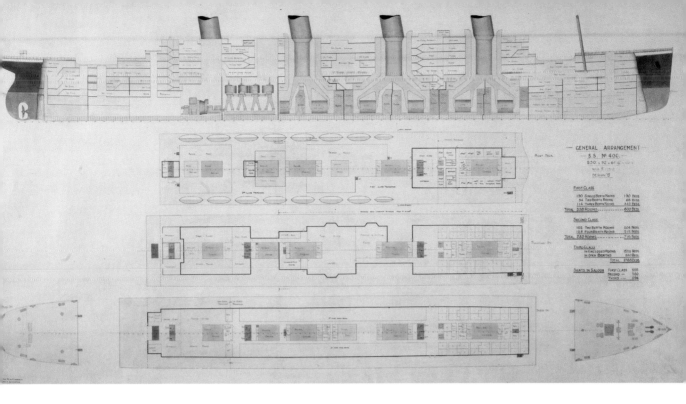

Original design drawings for *Olympic* and *Titanic* approved on 29th July 1908 by Bruce Ismay and other White Star Line directors.

Bruce Ismay,
Chairman of the White Star Line

The Decision

At his London residence in the summer of 1907, William Pirrie had a discussion over dinner with Bruce Ismay. They looked at the challenge presented to the White Star Line's north Atlantic passenger service by the Cunard Line's new large, fast ships *Lusitania* and *Mauretania*. Their decision that Harland & Wolff should build three enormous vessels for the White Star Line led to the creation of the famous *Titanic* and her sister ships.

Preliminary designs were soon under way and work began to prepare the shipyard for the task. By July 1908, General Arrangement drawings had been completed at Harland & Wolff and these were approved on 29 July 1908 by Bruce Ismay and other White Star Line directors. This approval allowed detailed design drawings to be prepared for the new Olympic Class ships.

William Pirrie,
Chairman of Harland & Wolff

Lord Pirrie

'On a site without natural advantages, where all the fuel and material required have to be imported, he has raised up a colossal concern which gives employment to between 14,000 and 15,000 men, and pays out in wages over £25,000 a week.'

Syren & Shipping, 28 June 1911

William Pirrie was apprenticed to Harland & Wolff in 1862, becoming chairman in 1895. His undoubted talents in shipbuilding, innovative design and financial management ensured that the company developed and expanded. By 1911, the firm was one of the largest shipbuilders in the world.

Pirrie was active in wider commercial and political circles, serving as Lord Mayor of Belfast in 1896-1897. His medals reflect the extensive network of organisations with which he was associated.

Vanity Fair cartoon of William Pirrie by renowned artist Sir Leslie Matthew Ward, known as 'Spy'.

Belfast and the Province of Ulster

William Pirrie's Ormiston House in Belfast shown left. Originally built in 1865-67 for James Combe, it was purchased by Edward Harland in 1880 and from 1887 belonged to William Pirrie. Pirrie extended the property in 1896-97 when he was Lord Mayor of Belfast. Ormiston House later passed into the ownership of Harland & Wolff and from 1928 until the mid-1970s it belonged to Campbell College.

Institution of Mechanical
Engineers badge, inscribed:
'The Institution of Mechanical
Engineers, Belfast, 1912'.

New Zealand Mechanical
Engineers gold Maltese Cross,
inscribed: 'Presd. to Lord Pirrie
by N.Z. Engineers, Life Hon.
Associate, Jan. 1907'.

Belfast Harbour Commissioner's
badge. William Pirrie was an active
member of the Belfast Harbour
Commissioners.

Institution of Mechanical
Engineers badge.

Institute of Journalists badge
showing the arms of Ulster and
the arms of Belfast. It is inscribed:
'Institute of Journalists, Ulster
Dist. Conference Belfast, 1896'.

Institution of Mechanical
Engineers badge, inscribed:
'The Institution of Mechanical
Engineers, Cambridge 1913'.

Shipwrights Company Past
Masters badge, inscribed:
'The Rt. Hon. Lord Pirrie K.P.
Master, 1909-10'.

Queen Victoria Jubilee medal, 1897,
given to city mayors to commemorate
the Diamond Jubilee.

The floating crane was used to lift heavy equipment and machinery on board ships at the fitting-out berth.

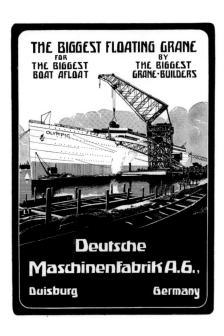

Preparing the Yard

Building ships on the scale of *Olympic*, *Titanic* and *Britannic* presented huge challenges to Harland & Wolff. The new ships required special facilities to cater for their size.

William Pirrie lobbied the Belfast Harbour Commissioners to construct the Thompson Graving Dock, the largest in the world at that time. Work began in 1904 and was completed in time for the dry docking of *Olympic* on 1 April 1911. Costing about £350,000, its construction was delayed by the partial collapse of the adjacent Alexandra Dry Dock.

New slipways, an enormous gantry and a huge crane were put in place to allow for the efficient construction of the ships. The steel gantry was built in 1908 at a cost of £100,000. Supplied by Sir William Arrol & Company of Glasgow, it carried the cranes and lifts for constructing the hulls. A floating crane, the largest of its kind, was imported from Germany.

This huge investment was justified by the close working relationship with the shipowners, the White Star Line. Since the 1870s Harland & Wolff had built every White Star liner.

The construction of the Olympic Class ships showed how well Harland & Wolff succeeded in this enormous enterprise.

The Arrol gantry and equipment stood at 228 feet (69 metres) high and 840 feet (256 metres) long.

View from *Olympic* of the recently completed Thompson Graving Dock. In the distance, *Titanic* can be seen under construction beneath the gantry. The dry dock was 850 feet (259 metres) long but could be extended by nearly 38 feet (11.5 metres) by repositioning the caisson gate. It still survives but is no longer in use.

Harland & Wolff shipyard, Belfast, 1911

Harland & Wolff Shipyard

'Preparations for construction
and launching ... were undertaken
upon a costly and magnificent scale.'

Belfast News Letter, 21 October 1910

This illustration shows Harland & Wolff's extensive shipyard when the *Titanic* and her sister ships were under construction. Their hulls were built on two slipways surmounted by the impressive Arrol gantry in the centre of this image.

Smaller slipways can be seen to the right, near the platers' sheds. Just above and to the right of the Arrol gantry are the machine and joiners' shops as well as the drawing, main and time offices. On the other side of Queen's Road, to the right, are Harland & Wolff's boiler and foundry works as well as the areas where carpenters, joiners, upholsterers and sailmakers plied their trades.

The dark, smoky area behind the Arrol gantry is the engine works of the shipbuilding firm of Workman Clarke. Their shipyard can be seen to the left of the gantry.

On the waterfront, to the left, are the pumping house and graving (dry) docks. A single funnelled vessel sits in the furthest of the graving docks, the Thompson Dock, used for the Olympic class ships. One of these can be seen beside the huge crane on the extreme left. The floating crane was used to lift heavy equipment and machinery on board *Olympic*, *Titanic* and *Britannic* when they were docked at the fitting-out berth.

The facilities at Harland & Wolff were in a constant state of change and development, as the shipyard adapted to requirements over the years. The Arrol gantry remained in use until the 1960s and the Thompson Graving Dock was utilised until 2002.

Drawing Office

The Drawing Office at Harland & Wolff was where the design of Olympic Class ships was worked out in intricate detail. Building on years of expertise in ship design, every aspect of the ships' construction was carefully considered and set out in the drawings. A ship was only drawn once, so the plans for *Olympic* were also used for *Titanic* and any changes and improvements were duly noted.

Ships' plans were often very long and highly detailed, so large, well-lit drawing desks were required for ease of working. The design of the Olympic Class ships owed much to Alexander Carlisle who retired as chief draughtsman in 1910, the Chairman William Pirrie and Thomas Andrews who was head of the Naval Architects' Department at Harland & Wolff.

Boat Deck on *Olympic*, pictured during the fitting out of the ship in 1911. This deck was the highest on the ship and was mainly used by passengers for leisure activities.

Upper Decks

The Olympic Class General Arrangement plan, opposite, shows the upper decks of *Olympic*. It also shows the location of accommodation, dining facilities, stairways and public areas on board the ship.

From this plan various booklets and other plans of the passenger accommodation were produced for use by the White Star Line or its agents to sell accommodation to passengers. This is an early plan for *Olympic* and there were some changes and improvements made for the layout of *Titanic*.

Promenade Deck on *Olympic*, May 1911. The Verandah and Palm Court cafes can be seen in the foreground. This deck contained facilities for First Class passengers, including a lounge, reading and writing room, smoke room and staterooms. Outside, the extensive deck space was attractive for walking or relaxing on deck chairs.

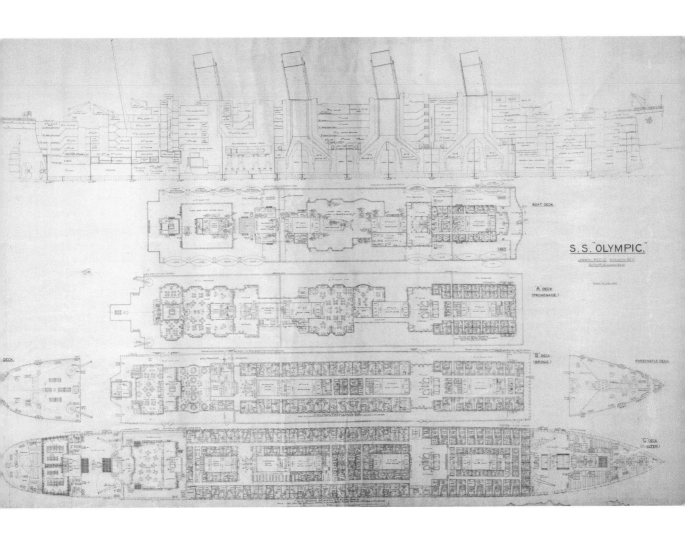

S. S. "OLYMPIC."

BOAT DECK

"A" DECK
(PROMENADE)

"B" DECK
(BRIDGE)

FORECASTLE DECK

"C" DECK
(SALOON)

The rigging plan for *Olympic* is shown below. Note the drawing amendments to the funnels showing how their overall height was lowered at an advanced design stage. This was done to give the Olympic Class ships a more impressive and sleek appearance. The fourth funnel was not required to ventilate the boilers, but did supply fresh air to the engine rooms and kitchens. It also gave the impression of more power and speed to those passengers who judged ships by the number of funnels they carried.

This drawing was produced in the Drawing Offices at Harland & Wolff for use by the Rigging Shop. Yard workers, called riggers, installed equipment such as the wire and fibre ropes that supported the masts and funnels. They also rigged the wireless antenna between the ship's fore and aft funnels.

Funnel Power

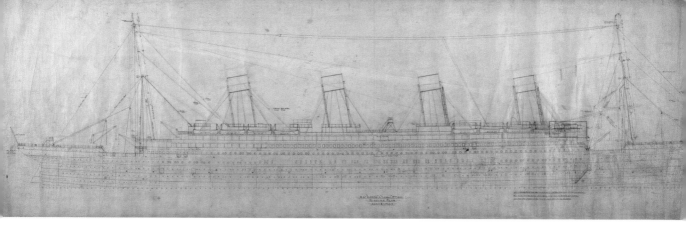

Half-hull model showing the original height of the funnels. The model was photographed in the Drawing Offices at Harland & Wolff.

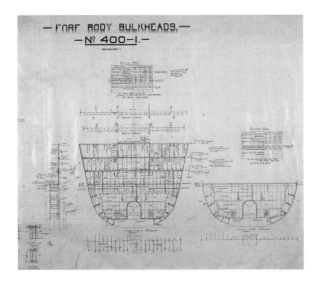

Bulkheads

Bulkhead plan, left, with the yard numbers for *Olympic* (400) and *Titanic* (401) shown in the heading.

Bulkheads are transverse steel walls that divide a ship's hull into watertight compartments. *Olympic* and *Titanic* each had fifteen bulkheads, but they did not extend to the full height of the hull. The design was such that any two compartments could be flooded without affecting the safety of the ships. If more than two compartments flooded, water would flow over the top of one bulkhead and flood the adjacent compartment.

Single watertight door in the open position.

Watertight door in the closed position.

Building Ships

By late 1910 the interior of *Titanic* was starting to
take shape. The image above shows the steel beams
and hatchways of the upper decks being fixed in place.
Note the wooden supports under the steel beams.

Taken on 30 July 1909, this photograph shows the early stages in the construction of *Olympic* (in the foreground) and *Titanic*. *Olympic's* double bottom is in place and the tank top is being plated. The worker, lower left, gives an idea of the scale of the ship.

The sister ships pictured shortly before the launch of *Olympic* (right) in October 1910.

Olympic fitting out at the deepwater wharf. The two gangways were used by the workers as they installed the engines, boilers, funnels and the many items of equipment and furnishing. The floating crane lifted heavy items on board.

Titanic photographed shortly before her launch on 31 May 1911, with the viewing stand in place just beyond the bow. The ship's name has been enhanced by the photographer. In the foreground can be seen the access ramps for the gantry. These ramps were used by the thousands of workers during the construction of the Olympic Class ships.

This iconic picture shows workers fitting the starboard (right) tailshaft on *Titanic*. The image of one employee, standing on the right, has been removed by the photographer but traces still remain. The Darlington Forge Company produced the rudder which can be seen on the left.

One of *Titanic's* reciprocating engines pictured in the Harland & Wolff Engine Works.

Steam Power

The Olympic Class ships were powered by two conventional triple expansion reciprocating steam engines working in combination with a low pressure steam turbine. This combination had been installed in the White Star Line's *Laurentic*, which came into service in 1909. *Laurentic* proved more efficient to operate than her sister ship, *Megantic*, which had conventional quadruple expansion engines. The success of *Laurentic's* engines led to the same combination being used in the Olympic Class ships and other vessels.

Employees working on the turbines for *Britannic* in the Engine Works.

Shipbuilding & Engineering Works

Belfast 21st July, 1911

Captain McIntyre,
Harbour Master,
BELFAST.

Dear Sir,

No. 401 s.s. "Titanic".

No doubt it has been reported to you that one of the cross channel steamers passed the above vessel about 12.15 p.m. yesterday, at a high rate of speed, causing the "Titanic" to range heavily on her moorings, and one of the 5" long fore and aft springs parted, causing the wire hawser to fall suddenly on one of the scows on which several men were working, which, of course, was most dangerous, as some of the men narrowly escaped being killed and knocked into the water.

We may further say that recently we have observed that the mid-day channel steamers frequently pass this vessel at too high a rate of speed, which was especially the case when these Works were closed for holidays last week.

We shall be glad if you will please take the necessary steps to prevent a recurrence, and we shall be glad to have your assurance accordingly.

Yours truly,

For HARLAND & WOLFF LTD.

BELFAST HARBOUR COMMISSIONERS.

HARBOUR MASTER'S OFFICE,
BELFAST, *22nd July, 1911.*

EXCESSIVE SPEED OF STEAMERS IN THE HARBOUR.

Several complaints have been received lately in regard to the excessive speed of steamers while in the Harbour more especially in the vicinity of the "Titanic" at New Deep Water Wharf.

The moorings of that steamer have been carried away twice, and yesterday several men narrowly escaped being killed by a wire mooring parting above where they were working.

Please be good enough to caution the masters of your vessels to exercise every precaution, and go slow, while navigating in the Harbour to prevent injury to life and property.

J. M'INTYRE,
Harbour Master.

Excessive Speed

In the early twentieth century, Belfast was an extremely busy port and there was considerable traffic entering and leaving the harbour. Steamships travelling at speed caused a wash that could reach nearby vessels, including those at the deep water wharf. Even ships as large as *Titanic* could be affected as is seen in the above letter of 21 July 1911 which describes a potentially dangerous incident. The Belfast Harbour Commissioners quickly responded to the complaint from Harland & Wolff and issued an official notice the next day.

The cross-channel steamer most likely to have caused the problem in 1911 was the *Viper*, a turbine steamer that made daily crossings between Belfast and the Clyde.

The cross-channel ferry *Viper* steaming past *Titanic's* sister ship *Britannic* at the fitting out wharf.

Sacks of rivets stored by Harland & Wolff. Approximately three million rivets, weighing an estimated 1,500 tons, were used in the construction of *Titanic*.

Rivet hammer used to strike newly inserted, rapidly cooling rivets to secure them tightly. Riveters hammered in pairs, striking the rivet alternately. It was very noisy work.

Riveting

The steel structures of Olympic Class ships were riveted together. Most of this was carried out by hand, but hydraulic riveting machinery was also used.

Hand-riveting was undertaken by a team of three men and one or two young boys. Each squad was allocated a certain section of plating. Rivets were heated in portable furnaces until they were white hot. A boy then carried the rivet in tongs to where it was needed and it was inserted into a hole through the steel plates. One man used a special hammer to 'hold up' the rivet while two riveters, on the other side, hammered it to secure it tightly as it cooled. Work would be closely inspected

and if any loose rivets were found they would have to be removed and the process started all over again.

Hydraulic riveting machines were difficult to manoeuvre in confined spaces and could only be used on level, uninterrupted plating. This type of riveting was well established at Harland & Wolff when *Olympic* and *Titanic* were under construction. Comparison tests in the 1910s showed that in some cases hydraulic-riveted work was weaker than that produced by hand-riveting. The main benefit of hydraulic riveting was the saving in time and labour.

Hand riveters working on *Titanic's* sister ship, *Britannic*, 1913.

Cluan Place terraced houses, originally built in 1884 in east Belfast, but now part of Ballycultra Town at the Ulster Folk & Transport Museum. One of these houses was the home of Bob Carlisle, a riveter at Harland & Wolff.

Hydraulic riveting work on vertical keel plates. The machines were suspended from travelling cranes running along the Arrol gantry.

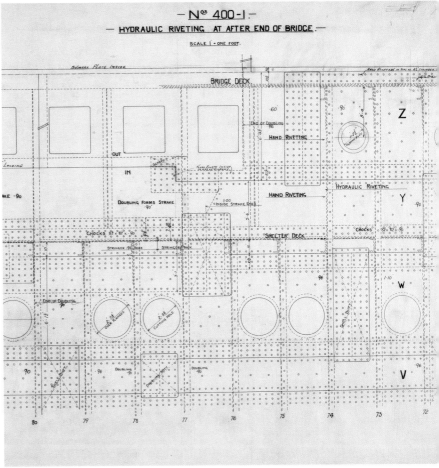

Hydraulic riveting plan for *Olympic* (yard number 400) and *Titanic* (yard number 401).

Building Lifeboats

Harland & Wolff constructed many of the lifeboats that were carried on the yard's ships. The Olympic Class lifeboats were designed by Chief Draughtsman Roderick Chisholm, who lost his life in the *Titanic* disaster. Sixteen of the twenty lifeboats on *Titanic* were built in Belfast. The largest boats were 30 feet (9.1 metres) long and could carry sixty-four people. The smallest ones were 25 feet (7.6 metres) in length and held thirty-three people.

Tool chest owned by a Harland & Wolff shipwright who built lifeboats. The chest contains a caulking mallet and various caulking irons, used to drive fibres into the seams in wooden boats to make them watertight.

Harland & Wolff shipwrights constructing lifeboats.

Shipwrights using adzes at Harland & Wolff.

Working with Wood

The Harland & Wolff shipyard had a highly skilled workforce. Working with wood was particularly important in shipbuilding and required a wide range of tools. Amongst the most important was the adze, a type of axe that was used to smooth or carve rough wood.

A shipwright's adze.

Workers used their own tools in the shipyard.
This adze is marked with the owner's initials.

Creating Interiors

This chair, shown left, from the Second Class dining saloon on *Olympic* is identical to ones that were on board her sister ship *Titanic*. The chair is made from mahogany, carved in Art Nouveau style and mounted on a cast iron base.

These and other chairs on board were made by Harland & Wolff. The above photograph of the company's store of assorted cast iron bases reveals the scale of the operation. These bases could be produced in great numbers, but used with different types and styles of chair. The upholstery for chairs and other soft furnishings required on board ships were made by skilled women in workshops at Harland & Wolff, shown below.

Cabinetmakers

The cabinetmakers' workshop, shown left, at Harland & Wolff was where skilled craftsmen built the wooden furnishings for fitting on board ship. Cabinetmakers served long apprenticeships before they were allocated their own bench. They also built up their own set of tools, sometimes inheriting them from a father or other relation who had worked in the same trade in the yard.

Cabinetmakers were amongst the most highly skilled and well paid workers at Harland & Wolff. In the early twentieth century, a cabinetmaker earned about thirty-three shillings and nine pence per week. The highest paid workers were plumbers, earning a weekly wage of thirty-six shillings.

This photograph shows the cabinetmakers in the foreground making a type of fitted furniture called a compactom. This provided washing facilities in cabins, with a tank behind the centre mirror supplying water to a basin. The basin could then be tipped up, pouring the used water into a galvanised container in the bottom of the compactom. The double compactoms shown were being made from various softwoods and faced with the finest mahogany, typical of the pattern fitted in *Olympic* and *Titanic's* First and Second Class cabins.

An artist's illustration showing an Olympic Class stateroom (First Class cabin), with furnishings made by Harland & Wolff.

Timber store in Harland & Wolff.

A Grand Staircase

This carved oak panel is from a newel post on the Grand Staircase of *Olympic*. The beautiful design and craftsmanship was inspired by the work of seventeenth century master carver Grinling Gibbons. An identical panel, now in the Maritime Museum of the Atlantic, in Nova Scotia, Canada, was retrieved from the water after *Titanic* sank.

View of the Grand Staircase on *Olympic*, highlighting the elaborate decorative wood carvings such as the panel (left).

Men who built Titanic

Around 15,000 people were employed by Harland & Wolff when *Titanic* and her sister ships were under construction. They lived and worked in an atmosphere of heightened political and religious tensions associated with support for, and opposition to, Home Rule for Ireland. Most lived in east Belfast and many travelled to and from work by tram. There were close community links with the shipyard which often employed several members of a family, spread across two or more generations.

The above photograph shows just some of the workers at Harland & Wolff. Note that nearly all are wearing a flat cap. Known as a 'duncher', this was an essential part of the working man's everyday dress.

Timekeeping

Harland & Wolff timekeeping boards.

At Harland & Wolff timekeeping boards were used to keep track of the hours that the employees worked. Each wooden timekeeping board was stamped with the number of a worker. The Time Office would issue them to workers when they 'clocked in'. The board was returned by employees when they 'clocked out', allowing the correct wages to be calculated for each day's work. Staff in the Time Offices kept a careful record of each employee and the hours worked. The long line of buildings making up the Time Offices illustrates the facilities necessary in Harland & Wolff to monitor its large workforce.

Time Offices at Harland & Wolff showing the doors through which workers streamed each working day.

Life
On
Board

The White Star Line commissioned three nearly identical ships from Harland & Wolff and, between 1908 and 1915, the three Olympic Class vessels were built. The plan was for *Olympic, Titanic* and *Britannic* to work the lucrative north Atlantic route. The three ships were very large and built to the highest standards, with well designed accommodation for all classes of passengers. The White Star Line had vast experience in transporting passengers across the Atlantic and knew that their new ships would be a worthy challenge to the huge new liners, *Lusitania* and *Mauretania*, of the rival Cunard Line.

Yet although all three ships were built, the plan was never fulfilled. The second ship, *Titanic*, was to become world famous through sinking with huge loss of life on her maiden voyage. Her two sisters, *Olympic* and *Britannic*, are less well known and had very different careers. *Olympic* made her maiden voyage in 1911 and remained in service for a further twenty-four years. *Britannic*, like *Titanic*, was destined to have a short life. Less than a year after her maiden voyage in 1915, *Britannic* sank after striking a mine during the First World War.

Of the three ships, it is *Olympic* that best provides a window into life on board for passengers and crew. *Olympic* survived until 1935 when she was broken up and her fittings sold at auction. She was the most photographed of the three vessels, both because she was the first built and because she survived the longest. By understanding *Olympic*, we also understand *Titanic* because the two ships were almost identical and were built and fitted out within a year of each other.

Olympic (left) and *Titanic* together at Harland & Wolff, early 1912.

A Slice of Life

The three toast-racks reveal much about life on board the Olympic Class ships. The ornate toast-rack on the left was used in the First Class à la carte restaurant, where passengers paid extra for an exclusive dining experience. The centre toast-rack was designed for the First Class dining saloon, while that on the right was used in Third Class. Note how the racks cater for different widths of toast: à la carte was designed for the thinnest slices while the Third Class rack has the widest dividers.

These items illustrate how the social hierarchy of the time was reflected in the design of the Olympic Class ships. Not only did First, Second and Third Class passengers have specific sleeping, dining and public areas, but the items provided for their use were all designed according to where they were used on board. For passengers, this division simply mirrored everyday life on land.

On the Olympic Class ships, the type of service provided for all classes exceeded that in most other passenger vessels. In effect, all passengers travelled well.

English rose pattern china used exclusively in the restaurants on *Olympic* and *Titanic*. The OSNC interlocking letters stand for the Oceanic Steam Navigation Company, the official title of the White Star Line.

Superior Dining

A la carte restaurants were provided on Olympic Class ships. First Class Passengers paid extra for this exclusive dining experience in beautiful, elegant surroundings. From the start, the facility proved popular with the very wealthy passengers travelling on *Olympic*. This experience led to the decision to increase the size of the à la carte restaurant on *Titanic* to cater for the expected demand on that ship.

The à la carte restaurants were operated as private franchises, but remained under the White Star Line's overall management.

THE VERANDAH CAFÉ.

THE RESTAURANT; FURNISHED IN THE LOUIS XVI. STYLE.

Artist's illustrations of the elegant à la carte restaurant on Olympic Class ships. It was located on the Bridge Deck 'B'.

Silver dishes from the à la carte restaurant. The distinctive silver plate used in the restaurant was specially commissioned for *Olympic* and *Titanic* from the Goldsmiths' and Silversmiths' Company in London.

Illustration from 1911 of the First Class dining room on *Olympic*.

The First Class dining saloon on Titanic photographed by Frank Browne (later Father Browne) during his journey from Southampton to Queenstown. (© Fr. Browne SJ Collection/ Irish Picture Library)

First Class Dining

The First Class dining saloon on Olympic Class ships was located on 'D' deck and could seat 554 people at one time. It was decorated in early seventeenth century Jacobean style, with an elaborate plasterwork ceiling.

First Class passengers enjoyed a wide choice of dishes, choosing from specially printed menu cards. The standard of both food and service was very high.

Menu for the First Class dining saloon on *Olympic*, 11 August 1912.

First Class china used on Olympic Class ships. John Stonier & Company of Liverpool supplied most of the china used by the White Star Line. The china itself was made by a number of English manufacturers including Bridgewood, Wedgewood and Copeland Spode

First Class White Star Line cup, saucer and plate, with tea-strainer, teaspoon and knife.

First Class dish in 'Olympic' pattern. In 1911 the White Star Line commissioned Elkington & Company of Birmingham to design a new range of silver-plated tableware. The 'Olympic' pattern, with its series of lines with five-pointed stars, was designed especially for use in the First and Second Classes of the Olympic Class ships. The pattern was eventually extended for use throughout the rest of the fleet and was still in use in 1934 when the White Star Line amalgamated with the Cunard Line.

First Class fruit dish and grape scissors designed and manufactured by Elkington & Company. Elkington manufactured most of the silver-plated tableware used by the White Star Line from 1871 until 1934.

Second Class Dining

The Second Class dining saloon, located on 'D' deck, could accommodate nearly four hundred passengers.

The provision of Second Class travel reflected wider changes in society and the emergence of a growing middle class. Those travelling in Second Class on Olympic Class ships were provided with facilities that more closely resembled First Class on other ships.

The Second Class dining saloon, decorated in early English style, was normally laid out with long tables seating eight people. Passengers were offered a very good choice of food which, although plainer than in First Class, was of excellent quality.

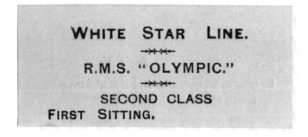

Olympic Second Class meal ticket. Sometimes passenger numbers made it necessary to have two sittings for meals in the Second Class dining saloon.

Second Class White Star Line Delft china plate.

Third Class passengers dined well on Olympic Class ships. Their dining saloon could seat about 473 people and meals were generally served in two sittings to cater for the large number of Third Class travellers on board.

Seated at long tables catering for up to fourteen people, Third Class passengers were provided with a menu for each day's meals. Food was plain, but plentiful, and was served by stewards. White cloths covered the tables and durable tableware was provided. The standard of food and service was remarkably good.

Third Class Dining

The Third Class dining saloon on 'F' deck was plainly furnished, but clean and well lit.

White Star Line Third Class place setting.

Third Class jug, bowl, cup and saucer, all clearly marked with the White Star Line name and logo.

Menu holder used in the Third Class dining saloon.

Jewish emigrants c.1910. In this period many Jewish emigrants to America came from central and eastern Europe. (Getty Images)

Special Tableware

The White Star Line catered for special categories of passengers, such as members of the Jewish faith who required Kosher food. China and silver-plated tableware was specially marked with either the words 'Meat' or 'Milk' in Hebrew and the food and tableware were prepared and washed in a separate part of the kitchen.

White Star Line tableware for Kosher food.

Crew Dining

Passengers on board Olympic Class ships were provided with different dining rooms depending on the class in which they were travelling. Similarly, different crew members had separate mess or dining arrangements. For example, there were separate messes for officers, engineers, seamen, firemen and greasers.

A separate dining saloon was also provided for the maids and valets of First Class passengers. Located on 'C' deck, it could seat up to forty-eight people. Nearby was a dining saloon for the Postal Clerks and Marconi operators.

Napkin ring marked for use in the servants' dining saloon.

Silver-plated dish stamped 'E.M.' for Engineers' Mess. Worn and damaged silver-plated tableware from First or Second Class was stamped and reused in either the Engineers' Mess (E.M.) or Officers' Mess (O.M.).

At Your Service

The White Star Line prided itself on the high level of service that it provided to its passengers. Stewards and stewardesses were assigned to serve First, Second and Third Class travellers, making sure that their journey was as pleasant as possible. Those serving First Class passengers often received generous tips.

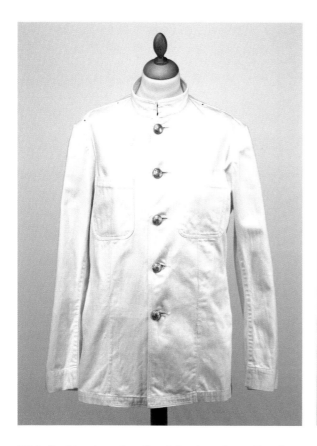

White Star Line steward's uniform belonging to George Russell, a steward for fifty-three years on White Star Line ships. He joined the company in 1903 and was serving on *Cymric* at the time of the *Titanic* disaster. The uniform has removable buttons to allow the garment to be boiled when washing so that it was as white as possible.

Apron for White Star Line stewardess, c. 1912. Made of cotton, it has silk White Star Line burgees at the shoulders.

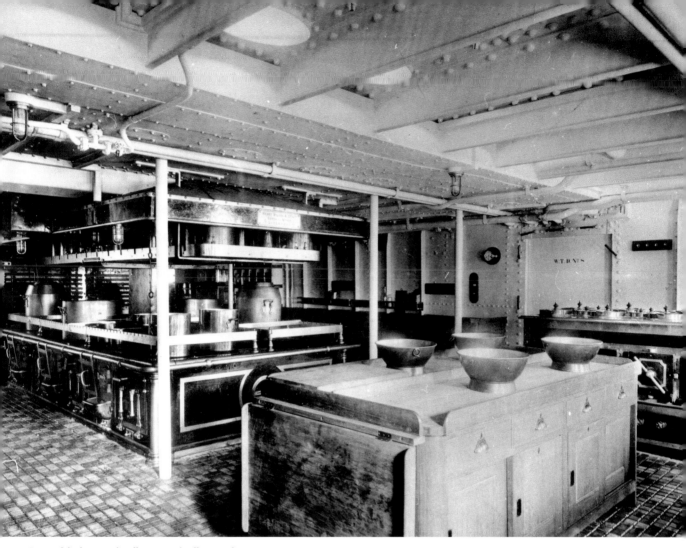

View of the large and well-equipped galley on *Olympic*.
Note the large pots on the stove.

Cooking on Board

Highly organised catering arrangements were needed to
feed both passengers and crew on Olympic Class ships.
There was a galley (kitchen) for First and Second Class
passengers, linked to pantries from which the dining
saloons were served. There were also separate Third
Class and crew galleys, bakeries and a butchers' area.

Large copper pots were essential when catering for the
thousands of passengers and crew on board Olympic Class ships.

Relaxing on Deck

This *Olympic* chair, from covered Promenade Deck "A", had a seat base originally upholstered with wicker in a herringbone pattern. The same design of chair, made entirely from wooden slats, was used on the open Boat Deck.

First, Second and Third Class passengers had access to different areas on board Olympic Class ships where, weather permitting, they could walk about or just admire the view. Enjoying the fresh air was popular with all travellers.

Several different types of deck chair, or steamer chair, were ordered for *Olympic* and *Titanic* for use by First and Second Class passengers on the Boat and Promenade Decks. Passengers paid a hire charge for each voyage of four shillings for the chair and the same amount for a woollen steamer rug.

Artist's impression of passengers relaxing on the Boat Deck on Olympic Class ships. Note the steward on the left who is serving refreshments to passengers.

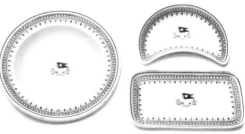

Special Deck Service chinaware was used to serve food to First Class passengers not taking meals in the dining saloon. Food could be brought to a cabin or stateroom, or could be served on deck. The same distinctive chinaware was also used by Second Class passengers requiring refreshment, such as beef tea, on deck.

The swimming bath, with dressing rooms and showers, was located on 'F' deck on the Olympic Class ships.

White Star Line silver tray and glass. The glass was probably used for serving port or liqueurs.

Letter card from *Olympic*. Writing letters on board ship was a popular way of passing the time on a long ocean voyage.

Leisure

Passengers occupied themselves in different ways to pass the hours. First Class passengers could use the Turkish baths, swimming pool, gymnasium or squash court, or could walk on deck if the weather was good. They also enjoyed playing cards, writing letters or postcards. Another popular pastime was listening to concerts provided by the musicians engaged to entertain the passengers on board.

Music booklet. The White Star Line provided music on board for its First and Second Class passengers. Concert programmes and other musical events were arranged on a regular basis.

Box of White Star Line playing cards.

White Star Line matchbox holders and ashtray. The Olympic Class ships provided smoking rooms for their passengers.

Design and Luxury

The variety of design and the high quality of craftsmanship, particularly in First Class, made accommodation on board Olympic Class ships both comfortable and attractive. The special staterooms on 'B' and 'C' decks were noted for their varied styles of decoration and their luxurious furnishings.

This sketch for a pair of walnut bed ends was made by Arthur Henry Durand. He designed many of the woodwork details on board both *Olympic* and *Titanic* and was part of a large team of designers who worked on the ships. These bed ends were made for a First Class Bedroom Suite.

First Class stateroom on *Titanic* showing the high quality of design.

Crystal glass and ormolu ceiling lamp from the First Class lift foyer on *Olympic*.

Illumination on Board

Vessels as large as the Olympic Class ships required a wide range of lighting on board. The electric lights varied in size and design, depending on their use and location. All fittings were of robust design to withstand the motion and vibration during ocean crossings.

Many of the lights were supplied by the London firms of Perry & Company and N. Burt & Company.

First Class lift foyer lit by crystal glass and ormolu ceiling lamp. There were three lifts available to First Class passengers, operating between decks A, B, C, D and E. A fourth lift was provided for the use of Second Class passengers.

A new innovation for First Class passengers was their own private promenade on *Titanic*.

The Adam-style sitting room on *Olympic*, part of the 'B' deck parlour suite.

'It is impossible to adequately describe the decorations in the passenger accommodation. ... They are on a scale of unprecedented magnificence. Nothing like them has ever appeared before on the ocean.'

White Star Line, 1911

First Class Staterooms

The White Star Line aimed to attract wealthy First Class passengers to its new Olympic Class ships and so it provided accommodation of the highest standards for these travellers. The First Class staterooms were located in the central part of the ship where motion was felt the least at sea. They were luxuriously furnished in a variety of styles and were beautifully decorated.

The two First Class parlour suites with private promenades were a new feature in *Titanic*. One was taken by Bruce Ismay, Chairman of the White Star Line, on the maiden voyage. The rate for First Class passengers was £660 during the "Intermediate Season" (1st April-31st July).

First Class parlour suite on *Titanic*.

Artist's impression of a Second Class cabin. This particular type could be converted to a First Class stateroom if required

Second Class Cabins

Second Class cabins on Olympic Class ships were well furnished and either two or four-berth in size. The four-berth cabins could serve as two-berth staterooms and some Second Class cabins could be adapted for First Class accommodation. Wardrobes were fitted in all the cabins, as were either single or double fold-up washbasin cabinets. Overall, Second Class passengers enjoyed comfortable, relatively spacious sleeping accommodation.

Third Class Cabins

White Star Line bed cover for Third Class cabins.

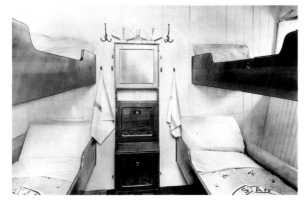

Third Class four-berth cabin on *Olympic* and *Titanic*.

Third Class accommodation on board Olympic Class ships rivalled Second Class cabins on other ships. Many Third Class cabins contained two berths, while four, six and eight berth accommodation was also available. The cabins were basic, plainly furnished and had washing facilities. This accommodation was an undoubted improvement on the very basic, dormitory type sleeping arrangements for Third Class passengers in other vessels.

Olympic and *Titanic* were each designed to carry over 1,000 Third Class passengers.

'Slops' bucket used in Third Class areas.

This enamelware jug was made by Richard Patterson and Company of High Street, Belfast. The jug is typical of the plain, robust and hard-wearing ware used to cater for Third Class passengers.

First Class chamber pot, often referred to as a 'vomit pot'. The design and size of *Olympic* and *Titanic* meant that passengers experienced seasickness less frequently than on earlier vessels.

A small number of First Class staterooms on Olympic Class ships had connecting private bathrooms, but most passengers had to use the public baths on board. These were provided for all classes, but Third Class passengers were only allocated two bathtubs: one for men and one for ladies. However, all passengers had access to washing facilities in or near their cabins.

Bathrooms on Board

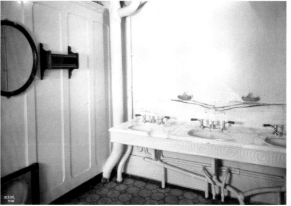

White Star Line notice relating to toilets on board ship. The Olympic Class ships provided flushing toilets for all passengers and crew.

Artist's impression of a First Class bathroom, part of the Parlour Suites on Olympic Class ships.

First Class public lavatory for gentlemen, on *Olympic*.

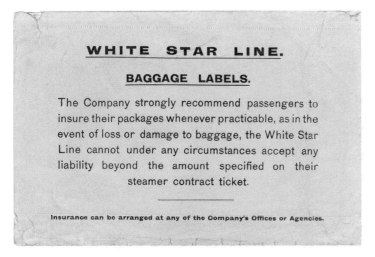

WHITE STAR LINE.

BAGGAGE LABELS.

The Company strongly recommend passengers to insure their packages whenever practicable, as in the event of loss or damage to baggage, the White Star Line cannot under any circumstances accept any liability beyond the amount specified on their steamer contract ticket.

Insurance can be arranged at any of the Company's Offices or Agencies.

White Star Line baggage labels used at the time of *Titanic*

Baggage

Passengers could have some of their baggage with them in their cabins, but other luggage was stored elsewhere on the ship.

Baggage labels ensured that the correct bags were stored in the relevant locations. Luggage that was required on board was usually marked 'cabin', 'stateroom' or 'wanted'. Items marked with 'baggage room' labels were stored in the baggage room where they could be accessed at set times during the voyage. Any items that were not needed during the journey were marked 'hold' or 'not wanted' and were stored in the hold of the ship.

Third Class luggage label, 1910s. The design had not changed when the label was reused by a Tourist Class passenger in the 1920s.

The Launch of Olympic

'The largest steamer in the world'

Olympic, the first of the three sister ships, was launched on 20 October 1910 in a blaze of publicity. Proudly proclaimed as the largest steamer in the world, Harland & Wolff spared no efforts to ensure that the world knew about her arrival. A specially produced launch booklet was prepared in advance and promoted the qualities of the new ship.

The ship's hull was painted light grey so that it would stand out better when photographed. Tickets were sold to spectators, with the proceeds going to the Royal Victoria Hospital in Belfast. Distinguished guests, including the Lord Lieutenant of Ireland (the Earl of Aberdeen), were joined by thousands of onlookers. Following the launch some of the guests were invited to lunch at the Grand Central Hotel, Belfast.

Such was the success of the event, that similar arrangements were used for the launch of *Titanic* on 31 May 1911.

Olympic launch booklet.

The launch of *Olympic* in October 1910. Following the launch, the seven-month process of fitting out the ship commenced.

LUNCHEON

UPON THE OCCASION OF

THE LAUNCH

..OF..

THE WHITE STAR LINER

"OLYMPIC"

(45,000 TONS)

THE LARGEST STEAMER IN THE WORLD

20TH OCTOBER. 1910.

GRAND CENTRAL HOTEL,
BELFAST.

MENU.

Huîtres au naturel.

Tortue Claire.

Turbot bouilli. Sauce Hollandaise.
Pommes naturel.

Petit Bouchées de Foie Gras.

Filet de Mouton à la Francais.
Pommes Olives. Choux de Bruxelles.

Punch à la Russe.

Faisan à la Brôche.
Salade.

Trèfle d'Orleans.
Meringues glacée Pralinée.

Dessert.

Café.

Special menu produced for the luncheon following the launch of *Olympic*.

Promotional postcard, issued before *Titanic* began service, showing *Olympic* at sea with her sister ship *Titanic* in the distance.

Olympic at Work

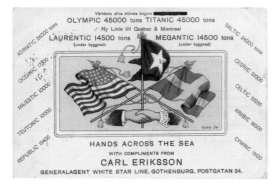

White Star Line agent's card advertising the fleet, including both *Olympic* and *Titanic*. Emigrants from across Europe travelled on White Star Line ships to reach America.

Olympic's maiden voyage, beginning on 14 June 1911, was the start of a busy career carrying passengers of all classes across the Atlantic.

The vessel's lavish First Class accommodation and her excellent Second Class facilities were soon popular with passengers. However, it was the lucrative Third Class market that was so vital for the profitability of the ship. Hundred of thousands of emigrants flocked to America from all parts of Europe in the years coming up to the First World War. They ensured that *Olympic's* Third Class accommodation was kept well filled in these years.

In October 1912, following the loss of *Titanic*, *Olympic* was brought back to Harland & Wolff where major work was carried out. This included extending the ship's double bottom up to the waterline, increasing the height of the watertight bulkheads and adding extra lifeboats. These and other improvements ensured that *Olympic* continued to attract passengers of all classes.

Olympic leaving the White Star Dock in Southampton on 24 April 1912, nine days after the loss of her sister ship *Titanic*.

Olympic, with its elegant lines, four funnels and powerful appearance, was popular amongst the travelling public.

Emigrants on the Poop Deck of *Olympic* passing the Statue of Liberty, New York.

Canadian troops boarding *Olympic* after the war, April 1919.

Engraved one shilling coin.

H.M.T. "OLYMPIC" LEAVING SOUTHAMPTON

"THE SHIP THAT BROUGHT ME HOME"

Left SOUTHAMPTON, June 7th ; Arrived HALIFAX, June 13th, 1919

1914 - Canadian Expeditionary Force - 1918

MONS	ST. ELOI	NEUVE CHAPPELE	YPRES 2	FESTUBERT	GIVENCHY	LA BASSE	LOOS
PLUGSTREET	ST. JULIEN	YPRES 3	THE SOMME	COURCELETTE	VIMY RIDGE	HILL 70	
PASCHENDALE	AMIENS	ARRAS	CAMBRIA	VALENCIENNES	OCCUPATION OF MONS, NOV. 11		

Postcard marking the return of troops to Canada at the end of the First World War.

Olympic at War

Olympic served as a troop transport during the First World War, initially during the Gallipoli campaign and later on the familiar north Atlantic service. From 1916 the liner was mainly engaged in transporting Canadian troops to Europe. From late 1917, after the United States entered the war, *Olympic* regularly carried American troops across the Atlantic. At the end of hostilities, the ship spent months bringing Canadians back to their home country. *Olympic* returned to Harland & Wolff in August 1919 to be refitted for regular passenger service.

Despite threats such as torpedoes and mines, *Olympic* came through the war without major difficulty.

Olympic in dazzle paint camouflage during the war.

On 12 May 1918, off south-west England, *Olympic* rammed and sank the German submarine U-103, shown above. The destroyer *U.S.S. Davis* rescued about thirty of the submarine's survivors.

Olympic carrying troops across the Atlantic.

Olympic 1920s and 1930s

From the 1920s onwards, American immigration restrictions forced the White Star Line to develop modern facilities and new classes of accommodation to attract the leisure traveller. 'Tourist Third Cabin' offered the budget traveller better facilities than those found in traditional Third Class.

The ship was popular with passengers and ongoing improvements enabled her to continue in service until the 1930s. In 1934 *Olympic* was taken into the new Cunard White Star fleet, but made her last commercial voyage in March 1935. *Olympic* was broken up at Jarrow-on-Tyne in 1935 where many of her fittings were sold at auction.

A letter, dated 12 July 1921, provides a wonderful insight into life on board *Olympic* during a journey to New York. Signed 'Charley', the letter is addressed to the writer's grandmother and aunts in England. He enthusiastically describes life on board *Olympic*:

'You feel absolutely lost on a big steamer like this (the biggest afloat) especially travelling alone, but I soon got acquainted. I will try & give you some idea of the size of the steamer. It is almost 6 times larger than the one I came on from Mexico & that was not small, 4 times the length of the deck is a mile, has 3 elevators (lifts), all kinds of baths the most perfect I have seen, Turkish shower, electric, massage, light & swimming tank in which I take a swim every morning before breakfast; besides there is a gymnasium, a racquet court, number of reception halls (dancing, lounge, reading & smoking), 3 palm tea rooms, & an extra restaurant (besides the regular dining saloon) which is an additional cost, where top nobs go & don't want in common with the rest.

The general impression is that you are in a hotel & not on a ship. Every night we have dances, quite showy affairs, it is great sight to see the ladies' dresses adorned with pearls & diamonds, all trying I suppose to create the greatest sensation.

To-morrow at 12 a.m., we expect to land in N. York after having a most delightful time & pleasant voyage.'

Captain Walter Parker signed this photograph in 1929 for one of the passengers on board *Olympic*

Olympic resumed Atlantic passenger service after the war, sharing the route with *Majestic (II)* and the smaller *Homeric*.

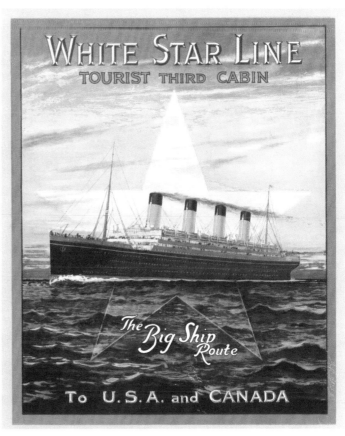

Posters and postcard advertising *Olympic* and the White Star Line, part of the International Mercantile Marine Company between 1902 and 1927.

The Old and the New

Titanic taking shape in the huge gantry at Harland & Wolff, with a sailing ship in the foreground. By the early twentieth century, the new technology of steel-hulled steamships was replacing the centuries-old tradition of using wooden sailing vessels to transport passengers and cargo.

Lord Pirrie (Chairman of Harland & Wolff) and Bruce Ismay (Chairman of the White Star Line) inspecting *Titanic* shortly before the launch.

Launching Titanic

Thousands gathered to watch the launch of *Titanic* on 31 May 1911. The public watched from every vantage point, while stands in the shipyard held ticket-holders including Harland & Wolff employees and journalists. Amongst the dignitaries present were J.P. Morgan of the International Mercantile Marine Company and Bruce Ismay, Chairman of the White Star Line.

William Pirrie, Chairman of Harland & Wolff, made a final inspection and, shortly after noon, gave the signal to launch. The hydraulic launching ram released *Titanic* and in 62 seconds she slid down the greased slipway into the water. The crowds cheered and waved in excitement. As was usual for White Star Line ships, there was no naming ceremony and no breaking of a champagne bottle on her bow.

The distinguished guests had lunch at Queen's Island, while others dined at the Grand Central Hotel in Belfast. As the crowds dispersed, *Titanic* was towed to the deepwater wharf for fitting out.

Over the next ten months *Titanic* received her engines, boilers, funnels and the thousands of fittings that transformed her into a magnificent ship ready for her maiden voyage.

Workman's launch ticket for *Titanic*, 31 May 1911. It was issued to a Harland & Wolff shipyard painter, David Moneypenny, who worked on the First Class accommodation in *Titanic*.

Distant view of the launch of *Titanic*.

Rare photograph of *Titanic* in the Thompson Graving Dock in Belfast
during fitting out. This particular photograph appeared in a newspaper
at the time of the tragedy, but has not been published since then.

The last time that sister ships *Olympic* and *Titanic* were together was in early March 1912. *Olympic* had returned to Harland & Wolff for repairs to a damaged propeller. This photograph shows *Olympic* (left) being manoeuvred into the flooded Thompson Graving Dock, with *Titanic* at the fitting-out wharf.

Two Sisters Together

THE NEW WHITE STAR LINER "TITANIC."

45,000 tons gross register.   66,000 tons displacement.   Built by Harland & Wolff, Belfast;
Accommodation, 2500 passengers and a crew of 860.   Speed 21 knots.   Estimated cost, £1,500,000.
100 feet longer and 12,500 tons more than the Cunard leviathans.   The following are the dimensions,
etc., of the great vessel :

Length over all .. .. 882 ft. 9 in.	Distance from top of funnel to keel .. .. 175 ft. 0 in.
Breadth over all .. .. 92 ft. 6 in.	Number of steel decks 11
Breadth over boat deck .. .. 94 ft. 0 in.	Number of water-tight bulkheads 15
Height from bottom of keel to boat deck .. 97 ft. 4 in.	Rudder weighs .. .. 100 tons.
Height from bottom of keel to top of captain's	Stern frame, rudder and brackets .. .. 280 tons.
house .. .. 105 ft. 7 in.	Each anchor .. .. 15 tons.
Height of funnels above casing .. .. 72 ft. 0 in.	Bronze Propeller .. .. 22 tons.
Height of funnels above boat deck .. .. 81 ft. 6 in.	Launching weight .. .. .. 27,000 tons.

WALTON, PUBLISHER, BELFAST.

Titanic postcards issued before the maiden voyage of the ship.

Promoting Titanic

Advertising and promotion were essential in keeping the White Star Line at the forefront of transatlantic passenger transport. The company encouraged public interest in the huge Olympic Class ships through many different forms of advertising including postcards and cigarette cards. Material advertising *Titanic* was quickly withdrawn after the disaster.

Collectable cigarette cards, featuring many different themes, were issued by tobacco companies to promote their products. This one refers to both *Olympic* and *Titanic*.

The Café Parisien on *Titanic*.

'... this café has the appearance of a charming
sun-lit veranda, tastefully decorated in French
trellis-work with ivy and other creeping plants ...'

The Shipbuilder, 1912

Café Parisien

The area occupied by the Café Parisien on *Titanic*
was originally planned as a separate promenade. The
decision was then made to furnish it in the style of a
French café, with trellis-work, plants and wicker chairs.
Meals and light refreshments were served to passengers
who sat at small tables and enjoyed the views from the
large windows.

Café Parisien was particularly popular with younger
First Class passengers. A similar café was later added
to Olympic.

English rose pattern teapot from *Olympic*, used in the Café Parisien.

Photograph showing the Southampton incident when suction from *Titanic's* propellers snapped the mooring lines of the steamer *New York*, drawing her stern towards *Titanic*. Fast action by *Titanic* and nearby tugs narrowly averted a collision.

The Voyage

On 2 April 1912, *Titanic* sailed from Belfast to Southampton to begin her maiden voyage.

For over three years, the people of Belfast had grown used to seeing Titanic take shape in the Harland & Wolff shipyard. Sea trials were completed on 2 April and that evening *Titanic* left Belfast.

At Southampton coal and stores were loaded, the ship was made ready and on 10 April *Titanic* set sail. On board were just over 1800 passengers and crew. A near collision with the *New York* delayed departure, so *Titanic* was late arriving off the French port of Cherbourg. Specially designed tenders, *Nomadic* and *Traffic*, brought over 270 passengers on board.

Postcard of the White Star Line offices in Queenstown (now Cobh), County Cork. Queenstown was the last port of call for *Titanic*. It was the main place of embarkation for Irish emigrants and westbound steamships called regularly.

Letter posted from *Titanic* at Queenstown. It was written by Second Class passenger Herbert Denbury to his wife and describes the near collision with the liner *New York*. Denbury was travelling to New Jersey, but did not survive the sinking of *Titanic*.

'Dearest Ciss

It seems like old times to write the word *Queenstown*. We have had a good trip so far up till now you cannot feel her move . I don't know what she will be like later on I hope alright.

I suppose you saw in Wed night paper something about us nearly running in the America Line boat, the suction of these boats must be tremendous for the ropes of the other boat parted as if they were cotton. It was a good thing the tug was handy to take charge of her. Well dear, how are you. I hope you and the children are well. ... I think we will work it all right so dear, don't you worry, the parcel that went astray yesterday we found this morning so, so far every thing is all right. Bruce Ismay is coming with us. So I will let you know how things turn out later.

So sweetheart I will conclude with fondest love to you my dear sweetheart Wife & children Kiss them for me.

I remain your ever loving/sweetheart Husband Herbert

I hope I get a letter from you dear'

Card posted from *Titanic* at Queenstown by Second Class passenger Robert Phillips. He and his daughter Alice were travelling from Devon to a new life in Pennsylvania. The postcard was sent to a friend. Robert Phillips died, but his daughter survived the *Titanic* disaster.

This is one of the last photographs of *Titanic* and was taken by Frank Browne (later Father Browne) from the tender bringing him to Queenstown. He had travelled on the ship from Southampton. (© Fr Browne SJ Collection / Irish Picture Library)

The Loss of Titanic

Titanic left Queenstown on 11 April 1912 and headed west across the Atlantic.

The new ship made good progress and passengers enjoyed the excellent facilities. Her voyage was routine for her crew apart from a small fire in one of her coal bunkers that was brought under control after a couple of days. During the voyage several wireless reports warned of ice on her route. On 14 April at 11.40 pm, about 400 miles (640 kilometres) south-east of Newfoundland, *Titanic* struck an iceberg.

The damage caused by the collision was considerable. Six of her watertight compartments were opened to the sea. *Titanic* was designed to stay afloat with any two compartments flooded, but as the weight of water drew her down by the bow, water rapidly began to fill each compartment in turn. The pumps on board could only delay the inevitable. The ship was doomed.

The Marconi operators sent urgent distress calls and the Cunard liner *Carpathia* altered course and raced towards *Titanic's* last reported position. Captain Smith ordered the lifeboats to be swung out and filled with women and children. There were not enough lifeboats for everyone and many were not filled to capacity. When *Titanic* sank at 2.20 am on 15 April, over 1,500 lives were lost.

About two hours after the sinking *Carpathia* arrived and rescued 705 survivors from *Titanic's* lifeboats.

Lantern slide depicting the sinking of *Titanic*.

Cunard liner *Carpathia* was on route from New York to the Mediterranean when her commander, Captain Arthur Rostron, received *Titanic's* distress messages. His actions resulted in the rescue of 705 survivors.

These marine binoculars are from *Olympic*. On *Titanic*, the lookouts' binoculars were missing. However, this probably did not affect their sighting of the iceberg as binoculars are of limited use at night.

The White Star Line used the most up-to-date communication equipment on board *Olympic* and *Titanic*. Following *Titanic's* collision with an iceberg, wireless was vital in summoning help.

In 1896, Guglielmo Marconi had patented his wireless transmitting equipment and its value at sea was quickly recognised. First used on a transatlantic liner in 1904, the Marconi system had a daytime range of up to 400 miles (643 kilometres) and about 2,000 miles (3218 kilometres) at night. It was used to send and receive weather and navigation reports as well as passengers' private messages.

On *Titanic* there were two Marconi operators: Jack Phillips and Harold Bride. Using the old distress code CQD and the newer SOS, they alerted other ships to her plight. The exhausted Phillips did not survive, but Harold Bride was rescued. Rocket signals, Morse lamps and submarine signalling were also used to call for help from other ships.

Lantern slide depicting a wireless operator.

Marconi trade card showing the loss of *Titanic*.

Calling for Help

Wireless operator Harold Bride in the Marconi room on *Titanic*. Although the image is a double exposure, it is the only photograph of this important room. The photographer was Frank Browne (later Father Browne) who travelled on *Titanic* from Southampton to Queenstown. (© Fr Browne SJ Collection / Irish Picture Library)

Jack Phillips (left) one of two Marconi wireless operators photographed on board *Adriatic*. Phillips worked tirelessly to summon help when *Titanic* was sinking. (© Fr Browne SJ Collection / Irish Picture Library)

Titanic Crew

On her maiden voyage *Titanic* had about 900 crew on board. These included the Deck Crew of officers, quartermasters, able seamen and others, as well as the Engineering Department which included engineers, electricians and many firemen and trimmers. There were over 400 people in the Victualling Department, most serving as stewards or galley staff. In addition, the à la carte restaurant had its own staff and there were also postal clerks and musicians on board.

Many of the crew lost their lives in the disaster.

Jack Prideaux, born in Southampton, was one of the Third Class stewards on board *Titanic*. The 23 year old died when the ship sank.

Photograph of a young Joseph Boxhall. In 1912 he was 28 years old and was Fourth Officer on *Titanic*. Joseph Boxhall assisted passengers into the lifeboats before being put in charge of lifeboat number 2, leaving *Titanic* at about 1.45 am. He later gave evidence at both the British and American Inquiries into the sinking.

Captain Edward J Smith and his senior officers on *Titanic*, April 1912.

Left to right, front: James Moody (Sixth Officer), Henry Wilde (Chief Officer), Captain Edward Smith, William Murdoch (First Officer). Back: Hugh McElroy (Chief Purser), Charles Lightoller (Second Officer), Herbert Pitman (Third Officer), Joseph Boxhall (Fourth Officer), Harold Lowe (Fifth Officer).

Henry Wilde, Chief Officer on *Titanic*, took charge of loading the lifeboats on the port (left) side and was trying to release the collapsible boats when the ship sank. He did not survive.

Thomas Andrews

Thomas Andrews was born in Comber, County Down, into a prominent business family. Educated at the Royal Belfast Academical Institution, he began a premium apprenticeship at Harland & Wolff at the age of sixteen. He qualified as an engineer and became Managing Director and head of the Naval Architects' Department at the shipyard.

He was highly respected for his skills and enthusiasm in his work at Harland & Wolff. He contributed much to the design of *Titanic*, but the Olympic Class ships essentially were designed by Alexander Carlisle, who retired as chief draughtsman in 1910, and William Pirrie. Pirrie, Chairman of Harland & Wolff, was an uncle of Thomas Andrews.

Andrews travelled on *Titanic*, leading the Harland & Wolff Guarantee Group whose role was to address any technical issues that might arise on the new ship. Andrews' expert knowledge of the ship led him to quickly recognise that *Titanic* could not survive the damage caused by the iceberg. He remained on board the stricken vessel and died when it sank.

'The Titanic is now about complete and will, I think, do the old Firm credit tomorrow when we sail.'

Thomas Andrews, letter to his wife, 9 April 1912.

On 26 June 1908 Thomas Andrews married Helen Reilly Barbour. She was the daughter of John Dougherty Barbour of Dunmurry, County Antrim, who was prominent in the linen industry. They had one daughter, Elizabeth, born in 1910.

The Andrews Memorial Hall in Comber, County Down, commemorated Thomas Andrews. The hall was opened by his widow Helen in February 1915. Some of the funds were raised by Harland & Wolff workers.

Reverse side of the postcard of Rosa Abbott.

Signed postcard of Rosa Abbott.

Rosa Abbott

Rosa Abbott was a Third Class passenger on *Titanic*, travelling with her sons Rossmore (16) and Eugene (13). Born in England, she and her husband settled in Providence, Rhode Island in the United States, but separated in 1911. She then returned to England but her sons did not settle there and so they were returning to Providence on board *Titanic*.

The family ended up in the water when the ship sank and Rosa Abbott was pulled into collapsible lifeboat A. She was the only female passenger to be rescued from the water. She later transferred to collapsible lifeboat B, but suffered leg injuries from the cold water. Her sons did not survive.

The reverse of this photograph is inscribed: 'To dear Mrs. Lessman, in remembrance of the S.S. Titanic. April 15th 1912 Rosa Abbott, Survivor.' Mrs. Lessman was a passenger on board *Carpathia* when that ship rescued *Titanic* survivors.

The Cunard liner *Carpathia*, under Captain Arthur Rostron, that rescued *Titanic* survivors

Elsie Doling

Elsie Doling from Southampton was 18 years old when she was a Second Class passenger on board *Titanic*. She accompanied her sister-in-law Ada Doling on the journey to New York to visit Ada's mother.

When *Titanic* called to Queenstown, Elsie and Ada Doling were photographed while walking on the Promenade Deck. They were in the company of Edwin C. ('Fred') Wheeler, personal valet to George Washington Vanderbilt (who was not on board). Both Elsie and Ada Doling survived the sinking of *Titanic*, but 'Fred' Wheeler was lost.

Having been brought on board *Carpathia* from their lifeboat, the Dolings tried to send a Marconigram to Southampton saying 'Ada Elsie safe'. The heavy workload of the Marconi operators meant that it was not transmitted. Elsie Doling died in 1972.

Photographic postcard of Elsie Doling'. It is inscribed 'A Survivor from the illfated S.S. "Titanic" April 15/12'.

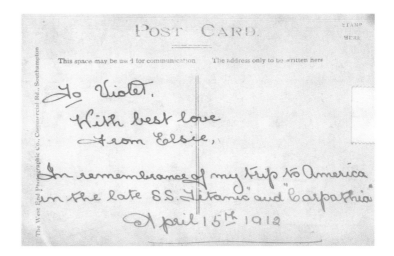

Reverse side of the postcard of Elsie Doling.

Elsie and Ada Doling strolling on *Titanic's* deck with 'Fred' Wheeler. The picture was taken at Queenstown by Thomas Barker, photographer for the Cork Examiner newspaper. He and other members of the press visited the new ship during her call to Queenstown. The photograph was subsequently published in the Cork Examiner.

The Marconigram from *Carpathia* which was never sent.

Lady Duff Gordon

Lady Duff Gordon was 48 years old when she travelled in First Class on board *Titanic* with her husband Sir Cosmo Duff Gordon and her secretary Miss Laura Francatelli. Born Lucy Christiana Sutherland, she was first married, at the age of 18, to James Stuart Wallace by whom she had a child. They were divorced in 1888 and she was left virtually penniless. She supported herself by establishing a dressmaking business - 'Maison Lucile' - in London. The 'personality' dresses of 'Lucile' were immediately popular. By 1900, the firm had become one of the great couture houses of London under the name 'The Maison Lucile.'

In 1900, she married Sir Cosmo Duff Gordon and they were on their way to New York on business when they boarded *Titanic* at Cherbourg, travelling under the names Mr. and Mrs. Morgan to avoid the press. Lady Duff Gordon and her husband and secretary were rescued in lifeboat 1 which had been launched carrying only twelve people (seven of whom were crew) despite having a capacity of forty. The couple subsequently gave evidence at the British Inquiry into the sinking; they were the only passengers who were called to testify. They rejected accusations that they had bribed the crew not to return to rescue people. They argued that the five pounds given to each of the men was compensation for the loss of their belongings. Lady Duff Gordon died in 1935.

Lady Duff Gordon in a publicity photograph of 1910. The original caption read: 'The latest photo of Lady Duff Gordon who has just arrived in New York with her bevy of beautiful mannequins who, it is reported, are taking the hearts of America's young men by storm. Lady Duff Gordon is, of course, the famous society woman who carries on the business of a dressmaker under the title of Lucile in Hanover Square, London. Lady Duff Gordon has just opened a branch establishment in New York.'

Four models outside Lucile Ltd. House in Paris in a photo shoot Lady Duff Gordon arranged to harmonise fashion and architecture. In April 1912 some of the Lucile models and other employees arranged a surprise 'send-off' for Lady Duff Gordon in Paris, giving her a bouquet of lilies-of-the-valley. She subsequently described looking at those flowers in her cabin on *Titanic* just before she left it for the last time. (Victoria & Albert Museum)

A curiously-named 1905 ensemble 'The Tender Grace of the Day that is Dead', by Lucile (Lady Duff Gordon).(Victoria & Albert Museum)

Evening gown called 'The Elusive Joy of Youth' by Lucile (Lady Duff Gordon), 1905. (Victoria & Albert Museum)

The Third Sister: Britannic

Britannic was under construction when the *Titanic* disaster occurred. *Britannic's* keel was laid down on 30 November 1911, but work on the ship was halted following the loss of *Titanic* in April 1912.

Major design alterations were made to improve the safety of the new ship. These included fitting a complete inner skin, increasing the height of bulkheads and fitting gantry davits to enable lifeboats to be launched from either side of the ship.

Postcard showing *Britannic* under construction at Harland & Wolff.

Launching Britannic

Britannic was launched on 26 February 1914 as the largest ship in the world, being slightly larger than her 'sisters' at 48,158 gross tons. The launch was meticulously organised and the huge ship entered the water without incident. It was planned that *Britannic* would begin transatlantic service in the spring of 1915.

Lord Pirrie, Chairman of Harland & Wolff, with dignitaries at the launch of *Britannic*.

A special booklet was published to commemorate the launch of *Britannic*. The ship was the largest British-built liner until *Queen Mary* was constructed for the Cunard White Star line in 1935.

Britannic shortly after her launch.

A Dream Denied

The dream of another magnificent Olympic Class ship was captured in this striking painting of *Britannic* by Charles Dixon. It depicts the ship in White Star Line colours in her intended role as a commercial passenger liner. The intervention of the First World War meant that this dream was to be denied.

Britannic: Hospital Ship

The outbreak of the First World War in August 1914
changed the future of *Britannic*.

The ship was in the course of being fitted out by Harland
& Wolff when war was declared. In November 1915
Britannic was requisitioned by the Admiralty for use
as a hospital ship. The vessel was adapted to carry
about 3,300 casualties, together with nearly 500
medical staff and 675 crew.

Britannic's maiden voyage began in Liverpool on 23
December 1915. Under Captain Charles A. Bartlett,
the ship sailed to the Greek port of Mudros, an Allied
base during the campaigns in that area.

In 1916 *Britannic* made several return voyages from
England to Naples and Mudros, bringing back thousands
of wounded soldiers. Most of the wounded occupied
public spaces on the upper deck. The intended First
Class dining room became an intensive care ward with
an adjoining operating theatre.

Some of the survivors from *Britannic* on board *HMS Scourge*. (Imperial War Museum)

The Loss of Britannic

On 21 November 1916, while heading for Mudros in sunny calm seas, *Britannic* struck a submerged mine laid by a German U-Boat near the island of Kea. The explosion disabled the automatic system for closing her watertight doors and the ship sank in less than an hour.

There were no wounded on board and just over 1,000 crew and medical staff were rescued from lifeboats by other vessels. Thirty people died when two prematurely launched lifeboats were sucked into the propellers.

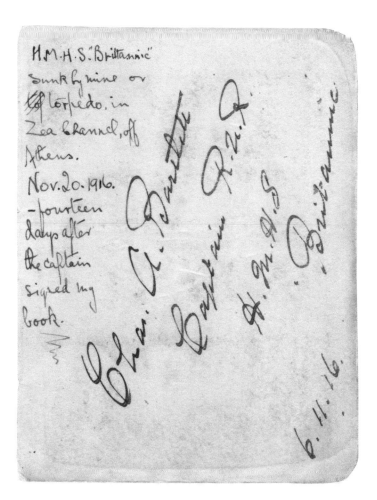

HMHS "Brittanic"
Sunk by mine or
torpedo, in
Zea Channel, off
Athens.
Nov. 20. 1916.
— fourteen
days after
the captain
signed my
book.

Page from a notebook with the signature of Captain Bartlett of *Britannic*, shortly before the ship was lost

Britannic on her final voyage passing the British flagship *Lord Nelson* at Mudros, Greece. (Imperial War Museum)

Titanic in Myth and Memory

CHAS·A·BUCHEL

The story of *Titanic* is a tale of two ships. The first ship was the actual vessel, designed and built in Belfast before sailing towards New York on its fateful maiden voyage. Its construction involved a network of people and places that straddled continents. This story is one of innovation, entrepreneurship and remarkable creative vision. It is also a tale of broken families and tragic loss of life.

The story of the second *Titanic* began as soon as the icy waters closed over the stern of the sinking ship. This is shown in our endless fascination with *Titanic*, the most famous ship in history, and how it endures in myth and memory. It is a story that has been dramatised in Hollywood blockbusters, but one that also lives in poignant local stories of pride and loss.

Since the tragedy, the ship's creation and destruction has been interpreted by generations of historians, writers, film makers, artists and others fascinated by the subject. It is a tale that can be adapted to reflect the interests and concerns of society. It gives rise to questions, discussions, myths and theories and the evidence is constantly being re-examined and analysed. This evidence includes not only the wreck itself, but the objects, photographs, survivors' descriptions and other material that survive from that era.

Today *Titanic's* sinking has come to symbolise disaster on a grand scale. Popular sayings such as 'it's like moving the deckchairs on *Titanic'* are part of our common language. Over the years it has become acceptable to use *Titanic* in ways that would have been inconceivable at the time of the tragedy. The image of the ship has become detached from the terrible events of 15 April 1912. *Titanic* has become a brand.

Photograph, taken in 2010, of *Titanic* mural on lower Newtownards Road, east Belfast.

Photograph, taken in 2010, of *Titanic* mural in Dee Street, off the Newtownards Road, east Belfast.

Belfast in Mourning

Belfast people were shocked and deeply saddened to hear about the loss of *Titanic*.

Harland & Wolff workers were stunned; they mourned the deaths of the nine members of the firm's Guarantee Group and the other local people who lost their lives. They also mourned the loss of the ship itself, the creation of which took such effort and skill. Their pride in *Titanic* was replaced with disbelief at how such a magnificent vessel could vanish so quickly.

The wider Belfast community also felt an enormous sense of loss, reflected in the holding of memorial services and other acts of remembrance and in generous support for the Titanic Relief Fund.

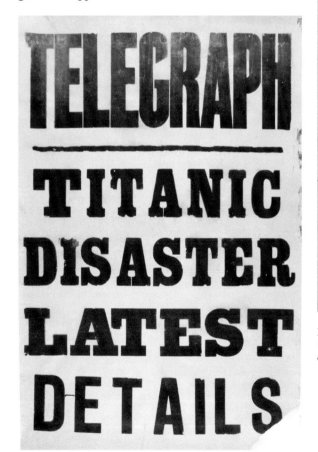

Notice used by the *Belfast Telegraph* newspaper to alert the public to the *Titanic* disaster. Shocked local people relied on the press for information about the tragedy.

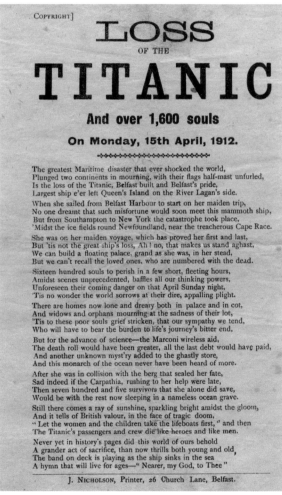

Poem, printed by J. Nicholson of Belfast, describing the loss of *Titanic*: 'Belfast built and Belfast's pride'. Many poems, songs and other tributes were published in the weeks following the tragedy.

Gymnasium on the *Titanic* showing, in the background, electrician William Parr, one of the Harland & Wolff Guarantee Group. He died in the disaster and was survived by his wife of two years and their baby.(© Fr. Browne SJ Collection/ Irish Picture Library)

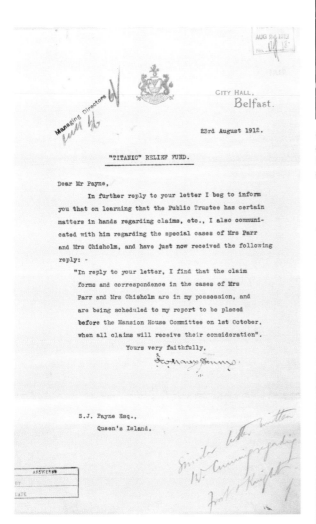

Titanic Relief Fund letter relating to members of Harland & Wolff's Guarantee Group, all of whom died on *Titanic*. This highly skilled group was on the new ship to address any technical issues that might arise. The letter mentions the widows of William Parr and Roderick Chisholm and, noted in pencil, the families of Anthony Frost and Robert Knight. Others in the Guarantee Group were Thomas Andrews, William Campbell, Alfred Cunningham, Frank Parkes and Ennis Watson.

Harland & Wolff employees gave generously to fundraising activities in the aftermath of the disaster.

One of many postcards issued after the disaster. Most featured an image of *Titanic*, together with text providing details about the ship and her maiden voyage.

In Memory of Titanic

The loss of *Titanic* led to many tributes to those who died. The dramatic news of the ship's sinking filled the newspapers of the time. Lists of those lost and saved, eyewitness accounts and endless speculation about every aspect of the disaster were eagerly read by the public.

Fuelled by this information, personal sorrow combined with public grief to create a demand for memorial material. Postcards, poems and music paid tribute to the bravery of those on *Titanic* and mourned those who died. Thousands attended special church services, fundraising concerts and the unveiling of permanent memorials. The nature of this public mourning revealed much about society at the time and laid the foundations for how *Titanic* would be remembered in the future.

Deathless Story was a special 'In Memoriam' issue of *Lloyds Weekly News*. It was written by the prolific author and journalist Philip Gibbs and published within two weeks of the disaster. It featured special 'inset' features on topics of special interest, such as 'The Titanic's Millionaires' and 'Death the Divider'.

Shipyard rivet punch inscribed 'SS Titanic lost Ap.15, 1912'

Souvenir programme from the Covent Garden 'Dramatic and Operatic Matinée' held on 14 May 1912 in aid of the Titanic Disaster Fund. Leading performers included French actress Sarah Bernhardt, English actor Sir Herbert Beerbohm Tree and Russian ballerina Anna Pavlova. Well-known public figures participated in many events aimed at helping those affected by the Titanic disaster.

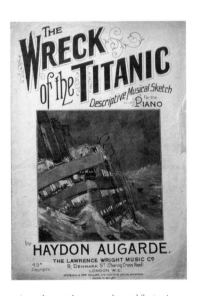

Musical tributes were paid to those who died in the disaster. Within weeks of the event, sheet music and records were released featuring music and songs dedicated to *Titanic*. These usually contained emotive and patriotic lyrics praising the bravery of those who died. Such tributes encouraged the public to donate to relief funds set up to help the families of those lost in the tragedy.

Lantern Slides

The series of hand-tinted slides, 'Loss of the Titanic, shown above and to the right, was produced in 1912. Slides such as these were designed for showing at public events when the images were projected onto a screen, accompanied by a narrator and music.

These slides portray the story of *Titanic*, beginning with the ship leaving Belfast, then showing the loss itself and finishing with images of a memorial service and a widow and children looking at a picture of the sinking ship.

The rapid production of these slides so soon after the loss of *Titanic* reflects the huge public interest in the tragedy.

Mourning Titanic

Postcards were very popular in the Edwardian period. They were a cheap and easy way for people to communicate with each other at a time when telephone use was not widespread.

This series of postcards was widely published. The images reflect the sense of loss and mourning after the *Titanic* disaster. Such cards, as well as being practical, were collectable at the time and have been since.

Nearer, my God, to Thee.
Nearer to Thee;
E'en though it be a cross
That raiseth me;
Still all my song shall be,
"Nearer, my God, to Thee,
Nearer to Thee".

Nearer, my God, to Thee, Nearer to Thee!
E'en though it be a cross that raiseth me;
Still all my song shall be,
Nearer, my God, to Thee, Nearer to Thee!

"NEARER MY GOD TO THEE."

In Memory

Many different types of memorials to those who died in the *Titanic* disaster have been created. Those dedicated to named individuals are perhaps the most poignant and recall the very real sense of loss experienced by those who knew them.

Plaque commemorating Abraham Mishellany, senior printer on *Titanic*, who was born in Lebanon but had settled in Liverpool. The ship had its own printing press to produce menu cards and other paper items used on board.

IN LOVING MEMORY OF
ABRAHAM HOLLAND MISHELLANY.
SENIOR PRINTER ON S.S."TITANIC"
WHO HEROICALLY PERISHED AT HIS POST WHILE
ASSISTING AT THE LIFEBOATS.
APRIL 15TH 1912.
"Thy will be done".
PRESENTED BY HIS WIDOW & OFFICERS & TROOP
20TH WEST LONDON B.P.SCOUTS.

Shown right, a decorated cello back plate paying tribute to the cellists on *Titanic*. The reverse is inscribed with their names and addresses, records that they were employed by C.W. & F.N. Black of Liverpool and refers to the memorial concert in London on 24 May 1912. All eight of the musicians on *Titanic* died in the disaster. They were reported to have played 'Nearer, My God, to Thee' as the ship sank.

An estimated crowd of early 100,000 people watched the unveiling of the memorial to *Titanic's* engineers in Southampton, 22 April 1914.

Public Memorials

There was huge public interest in the *Titanic* disaster and it is not surprising that the idea of commissioning permanent memorials soon arose. Generally funded by public subscription, memorials were erected in Belfast, Southampton, New York and many other places that had a link with the ship and those who sailed in her.

Titanic memorial, Southampton.

Photograph showing the Belfast *Titanic* memorial in its original location in Donegall Square North. In 1960 it was moved to its current position in the grounds of Belfast City Hall.

Photograph of the *Titanic* memorial lighthouse on the roof of the Seamen's Church Institute in New York. Funded by public subscription, the memorial was unveiled in 1913. Today it stands outside the South Street Seaport Museum.

A Night to Remember

The dramatic story of *Titanic* has been interpreted many times on screen. From the start, horror and grief were accompanied by a fascination with the ship. By August 1912 a German *Titanic* film, *In Nacht und Eis* (Night Time in the Ice), had already been made.

Other early films were produced, but it was not until the 1950s that there was renewed interest in the disaster. The 1953 film *Titanic* mixed fictional and actual characters. It was followed in 1958 by the influential *A Night to Remember*, a film praised for its accuracy and realism.

A Night to Remember was produced by Belfast-born William MacQuitty, who spent part of his childhood in Bangor, County Down. At the age of six, his father had brought him to watch *Titanic's* launch and he later recalled his emotion and pride in seeing the huge ship enter the water. His personal connection with *Titanic* fuelled his enthusiasm for the notable film which he produced over forty years later.

Public interest grew following the discovery of the wreck in 1985 and in 1997 the highly successful film *Titanic* featured remarkable special effects and accurate sets.

Titanic has much to attract film makers. It allows exploration of human stories set in the self-contained world of a luxury liner on its fateful maiden voyage. It uniquely captures a social order soon to be swept away by the events of the First World War.

The iconic 1958 film *A Night to Remember* was an adaptation of Walter Lord's 1955 book. Lord had interviewed sixty-three *Titanic* survivors and both book and film were praised for their accuracy.

Ticket for the premier of *A Night to Remember*.

The film *A Night to Remember* opened in a blaze of publicity on 3 July 1958 at the Odeon Cinema in Leicester Square, London. Several *Titanic* survivors attended the event. (Carlton Media)

Pictured at the premiere of *A Night to Remember* in July 1958 were (left to right): Sylvia Lightoller (wife of Charles Lightoller, Second Officer on *Titanic*), actor Kenneth More, the film's producer William MacQuitty and *Titanic* survivors Gus Cohen and Edith Russell.

Film programme, shown left and below, with signatures from the opening night. Those who signed were: Edith Russell (First Class passenger), Joseph Boxhall (Fourth Officer on *Titanic* and technical advisor on the film), Herbert Pitman (Third Officer on *Titanic*) and the actor Kenneth More who played Charles Lightoller (Second Officer on *Titanic*) in the film.

Discovering Titanic

The exciting discovery of the wreck of *Titanic* in 1985 led to renewed interest in the ship and her story. Although many had previously tried to locate the vessel, success went to a joint Franco-American expedition led by Jean-Louis Michel and Dr. Robert Ballard.

The wreck was located about 13 miles (21 kilometres) from its last reported position, sitting on the seabed approximately 2.33 miles (3.75 kilometres) below the surface. The discovery that the ship had broken in two was particularly interesting and confirmed some eyewitness reports of the sinking.

Ongoing exploration of the wreck helps to piece together information about *Titanic*.

Still photograph from the first television programme broadcast in the United Kingdom about the 1985 discovery of *Titanic*. It shows the manned deep-ocean submersible, *Alvin*, being brought on board ship. *Alvin* was used to explore and survey the wreck.

The bow of *Titanic* resting on the seabed. (© RMS Titanic Inc.)

A damaged tureen, marked E.M., shows that it was used in the Engineer's Mess or dining room. (© RMS Titanic Inc.)

This sides of the frame of this porthole were clipped to fit between between structural members on *Titanic*, so it probably came from a Third Class area. (© RMS Titanic Inc.)

Revealing the Past

These objects are just two of more than over 5,500 artefacts recovered from the wreck of *Titanic* by RMS Titanic Inc. As exclusive salvor-in-possession of the ship, the company's goal is to preserve and display these objects in memory of those who perished.

Since 1987 and 2004, RMS Titanic Inc. has conducted six research and recovery expeditions to the wreck. These expeditions are a collaboration of scientists, aquanauts, historians, marine archaeologists and engineers, naval architects and conservators from around the globe. Through this multi-national effort, knowledge of the ship and its passengers has grown, methodology for deep sea recovery and archaeology has been advanced and new artefact conservation techniques have been developed. The ship itself is slowly disintegrating and in time will disappear, but these and other artefacts bear witness to a once magnificent liner.

Such objects act as a poignant reminder of the human tragedy of the sinking. They were once part of everyday life for passengers and crew. Now, bearing the scars of their time deep on the ocean bed, they represent a link with the ship and all who built and sailed in her.

Titanic leaving Belfast Lough on sea trials, 2 April 1912. The ship faces the open sea and is destined to forge a remarkable place in world history.

A Century On ...

There are now no survivors left from *Titanic* but, a
century after her loss, public fascination with the ship
continues. The story of *Titanic* is a human and maritime
tragedy, but opens a window on a tale of endeavour,
innovation and industrial prowess.

Designed and built in Belfast, *Titanic* is part of a larger
story of technological progress, skilled workmanship
and entrepreneurship. Its legacy continues into the
future as generations discover anew the magnificence
of *Titanic* and the immense tragedy of her loss.

Select Bibliography

Bergfelder, Tim and Sarah Street, eds, *The Titanic in Myth and Memory: Representations in Visual and Literary Culture* (London and New York: I.B. Tauris & Co. Ltd, 2004)

Beveridge, Bruce, Scott Andrews, Steve Hall and David Klistorner, ed. by Art Braunschweiger, *Titanic: The Ship Magnificent: Volume One – Design and Construction* (Gloucestershire: The History Press, 2008)

Beveridge, Bruce, Scott Andrews, Steve Hall and David Klistorner, ed. by Art Braunschweiger, *Titanic: The Ship Magnificent: Volume Two – Interior Design and Fitting Out* (Gloucestershire: The History Press, 2008)

Gracie, Colonel Archibald, *Titanic: A Survivor's Story* (Gloucestershire: The History Press, 2008)

Howells, Richard, *The Myth of the Titanic* (New York: St. Martin's Press, 1999)

Lord, Walter, *A Night to Remember*, revised edn. (Middlesex: Penguin Books Ltd, 1987)

Louden-Brown, Paul, *The White Star Line: An Illustrated History 1869-1934, revised edn.* (Herne Bay, Kent: The Titanic Historical Society, 2001)

McCaughan, Michael, *The Birth of the Titanic* (Belfast: The Blackstaff Press, 1998)

MacQuitty, William, *Titanic Memories: The Making of a Night to Remember* (London: National Maritime Museum, 2000)

MacQuitty, William, *A Life to Remember* (London: Quartet Books Ltd, 1991)

McCluskie, Tom, Michael Sharpe and Leo Marriot, *Titanic and Her Sisters*, 2nd edn, (London, PR C Publishing Ltd, 2000)

O'Donnell, Dr E.E., *Father Browne's Titanic Album: A Passenger's Photographs and Personal Memoir* (Dublin: Wolfhound Press, 1997)

Acknowledgements

A publication of this kind inevitably involves contributions from many people, both internally and externally.

Special thanks must go to Alicia St. Leger for her research and scriptwriting services. Thanks also to Paul Louden-Brown for his expert input into discussions on Titanic and the White Star Line.

The richly illustrated nature of the book has been made possible by the patience and support of a number of colleagues in National Museums Northern Ireland, particularly our Photographic Department, namely Alan McCartney, George Wright and Michael McKeown. Invaluable curatorial and design assistance for collections photography was provided by Vivienne Pollock, Fiona Byrne, Fiona McClean and Heather Watters. Last but by no means least, the dedication and expertise of our Conservation Department has been indispensible and I would like to highlight the work of Joanne Lowe, Alison Muir, Lynn Stinson and JulieAnne Tolerton.

I am grateful to Una Reilly of the Belfast Titanic Society for kindly supplying the photograph of the premiere of 'A Night to Remember'. Finally, the following must be acknowledged for permission to reproduce images and photographs – Carleton Media, the Cork Examiner, the Fr Brown SJ Collection/Irish Picture Library, Getty Images, the Imperial War Museum, RMS Titanic Inc. and the Victoria & Albert Museum